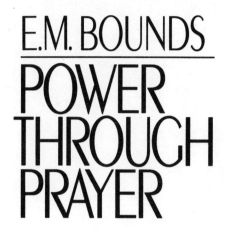

E.M. BOUNDS
POWER THROUGH PRAYER

E.M. BOUNDS

POWER THROUGH PRAYER

With Special Study Guides for Today's Reader

Edited by Penelope J. Stokes

World Wide Publications
A ministry of the Billy Graham Evangelistic Association
1303 Hennepin Ave., Minneapolis, MN 55403

Power Through Prayer, With Special Study Guides for Today's Reader

World Wide Publications is the publishing ministry of the Billy Graham
Evangelistic Association.

Scripture quotations are taken from the Authorized King James Version of
the Bible.

This special edition is published by the Billy Graham Evangelistic Association
with permission from the original publisher, World Wide Publications.

Library of Congress Catalog Card Number: 89-051181

ISBN: 0-89066-164-2

Printed in the United States of America

CONTENTS

ABOUT THE AUTHOR

Edward McKendree Bounds (1835-1913) was born in Shelby County, Missouri, where he studied law and was admitted to the bar at age twenty-one. After practicing law for three years, Bounds began preaching for the Methodist Episcopal Church, taking a pastorate at Brunswick, Missouri.

Imprisoned during the Civil War for refusing to take the oath of allegiance to the Federal government, Bounds later served as chaplain of the Fifth Missouri Regiment. He was captured and imprisoned in Nashville, Tennessee, and after the war pastored churches throughout the South.

E. M. Bounds is best known for his Spiritual Life Books, written from his home in Washington, Georgia, during the last seventeen years of his life. Bounds practiced what he preached; his own life was marked by a commitment to prayer, rising at four and praying until seven. His personal life of prayer and his writings about prayer have challenged and motivated Christians for generations.

ABOUT THE EDITOR

Penelope J. Stokes was educated at Mississippi University for Women and the University of Mississippi, receiving her doctoral degree in English Literature in 1978. She taught writing, literature, research, and speech at the college level for twelve years. During those years she developed and taught a course in Christian classics.

In 1985, Stokes left college teaching to pursue a full-time career in freelance writing and editing. Her articles and poetry have been published in such magazines as *Decision*, *Discipleship Journal, and Sunday Digest*. She is the author of several books, including *Ruth and Daniel: God's People in an Alien Society*, and World Wide's *Words in Season* devotional Bible study.

Stokes resides in Blue Earth, Minnesota.

Preface

In recent years the Christian church has seen a return to the classic works of devotional literature—the writings of people such as Brother Lawrence, Madame Guyon, Andrew Murray, and E. M. Bounds. Such men and women of faith have much to say to Christians of today; their commitment to Christ and call to live a holy and devoted life challenges us to move beyond the superficial routines of religion to a deep, life-changing, world-changing relationship with Jesus Christ.

The principles of prayer and holy living in E. M. Bounds's *Power Through Prayer* have significance to believers in every generation. Many of today's readers, however, find the more complex writing styles of earlier generations difficult to comprehend. The truths expressed by these giants of the faith are often obscured by the writing itself. This edition of Bounds's work, therefore, seeks to clarify the language to make these truths more accessible for today's readers.

In the original text, Bounds uses the generic term *men* to speak of those Christians called to ministry. I have generalized his usage, employing terms such as "believers," "Christians," and "men and women"—for all of us are included in God's call to be his representatives in the world.

In our generation, Christians realize that ministry happens in many contexts, including but not limited to the call to preaching and pastoral service. Where Bounds uses the term "preaching," I have substituted the more inclusive term, "ministry."

These editorial changes, along with the simplifying of Bounds's writing style, are intended to make the reading and understanding of the author's ideas more readily available to the reader. I have attempted to retain the color and flavor of Bounds's own style, and to maintain, at all costs, the integrity of his ideas.

Included in the text are additional notations: Scripture references for quotations and allusions to specific portions of the Bible; subheadings to divide each chapter into workable portions for group study or personal devotions; and application questions to help readers in thinking through and evaluating the significance of Bounds's ideas for their own lives and ministries.

Bounds himself said, "Prayer is the Christian's mightiest weapon. An almighty force in itself, it gives life and force to all." The universal impact of E. M. Bounds's *Power Through Prayer* continues throughout successive generations. As you read, study, digest, and apply the challenges he sets before you, may the same Spirit who empowered Bounds motivate you to a deeper, more intimate, more productive relationship with Jesus Christ.

Penelope J. Stokes
Editor

1

The Need for People of Prayer

Study universal holiness of life. . . . Give yourself to prayer, and get . . . your thoughts, your words from God. Luther spent his best three hours in prayer.

—Robert Murray McCheyne

System vs. Spirit

We Christians are constantly stretching to devise new methods, new plans, new organizations to advance the church and secure enlargement and efficiency for the gospel. This trend of the day has a tendency to lose sight of the individual, or to sink the individual in the plan or organization.

God's plan, however, is to make much of his people, far more of them than of anything else. People are God's method. The church is looking for better methods; God is looking for better people.

"There was a man sent from God, whose name was John" (John 1:6). The heralding of the way for Christ was bound up in a man—John the Baptizer. "Unto us a child is born, unto us a son is given" (Isaiah 9:6). The world's salvation comes out of a person—that cradled Son. And when Paul appeals to the personal character of the men and women who rooted the gospel in the world, he solves the mystery of their success: The glory and efficiency of the gospel is staked on the people who proclaim it.*

God declares that "the eyes of the Lord run to and fro throughout the whole earth, to shew himself strong in the behalf of them whose heart is perfect toward him" (2 Chronicles 16:9). He acknowledges the necessity of men and women, his dependence on them as a channel through which to exert his power upon the world. This age of automation is apt to forget this vital, urgent truth. But to forget it is as destructive to the work of God as striking the sun from its sphere. Darkness, confusion, and death would ensue.

What the church needs today is not new organizations or more and novel methods, but people whom the Holy Ghost can use—people of prayer, people mighty in prayer. The Holy Ghost does not flow through methods, but through men and women. He does not anoint plans, but men and women—men and women of prayer.

* The specific reference to this passage is uncertain, but several verses in the Pauline epistles point to the connection between the character of the messenger and the validity of the message. Philippians 1:27 exhorts those who speak the Word of Christ to let their "conversation" or behavior reflect the gospel of Christ. First Thessalonians 1:5-8 and 2 Timothy 3:10 refer to Paul's "manner of life" and the example he set for other believers.

Character

An eminent historian has said that the accidents of personal character have more to do with the revolutions of nations than either philosophic historians or politicians will admit. This truth applies to the gospel of Christ; the character and conduct of the followers of Christ can Christianize the world, transfiguring nations and individuals.

The character as well as the fortunes of the gospel is committed to believers. We make or mar the message from God to man. The Christian is the golden pipe through which the divine oil flows. The pipe must not only be golden, but open and flawless, that the oil may have a full, unhindered, unwasted flow.

Paul spoke of "my gospel" (Romans 16:25)—not that he had degraded it by his personal eccentricities or diverted it by selfish appropriation, but the gospel was put into the heart and lifeblood of the man Paul. It was a personal trust to be executed by his character, to be set aflame and empowered by the fiery energy of his fiery soul. Paul's sermons are mere skeletons, scattered fragments, afloat on the sea of inspiration. But the man Paul, greater than his sermons, lives forever, in full form, feature, and stature, with his molding hand on the church. The words he spoke are but a voice. The voice in silence dies, the text is forgotten, the sermon fades from memory; the preacher lives.

Living Words

The spoken word cannot rise in its life-giving forces above the individual. Dead people give out dead words, and dead words kill. Everything depends upon the spiritual character of the speaker. The Jewish high priest had inscribed in jeweled letters on a golden frontlet: "Holiness to the Lord." So must everyone in Christ's ministry be molded into and mastered by this same holy motto.

As Jonathan Edwards said: "I went on with my eager pursuit after more holiness and conformity to Christ. The heaven I desired was a heaven of holiness."

The gospel of Christ does not move by popular waves. It has no self-propagating power. It moves as the Christians who have charge of it move. The Christian must impersonate the gospel. Its divine, most distinctive features must be embodied in the believer. The constraining power of love must be evident, a projecting, eccentric, all-commanding, self-oblivious force.

The energy of self-denial must be the believer's heart and blood and bones. The Christian must go forth clothed with humility, abiding in meekness, wise as a serpent, harmless as a dove; in the bonds of a servant with the spirit of a king, a king in high, royal, independent bearing, with the simplicity and sweetness of a child.

Believers must throw themselves, with all the abandon of a perfect, self-emptying faith and a self-consuming zeal, into work for the salvation of others. Hearty, heroic, compassionate, fearless martyrs must be the men and women who take hold of and shape a generation for God. If we are timid timeservers, place-seekers; if we are people-pleasers or people-fearers, if our faith has a weak hold on God or his Word, if our denial is broken by any phase of self or the world, we cannot take hold of the church or the world for God.

Preparing Ourselves Through Prayer

As Christians, our sharpest and strongest preaching should be to ourselves. Our most difficult, delicate, laborious, and thorough work must be with ourselves. The training of the twelve was the great, difficult, and enduring work of Christ. Christians are not sermon makers, but saint makers, and we are only well-trained for this business if we have set ourselves apart for God's work. God does not need great talents or great learning or great preachers, but people great in holiness, great in faith, great in love, great in fidelity, great for God—people always speaking holy words, living holy lives. These can mold a generation for God.

The early Christians were of solid mold, after the heavenly type—heroic, stalwart, soldierly, saintly. Ministry with them meant self-denying, self-crucifying, serious, toilsome, martyr business. They applied themselves to it in a way that mightily affected their generation, and formed in its womb a generation yet unborn for God.

Real ministry is made in the closet of prayer; God's men and women are made in secret. Their lives and their profoundest convictions are born in their secret communion with God. The burdened and tearful agony of their spirits, their weightiest and sweetest messages come from time alone with God.

The church today is weak in praying. The pride of learning is against the dependent humility of prayer. Prayer is with the church too often only official—a performance for the routine of service. Prayer is not to the modern church the mighty force it was in Paul's life or Paul's ministry. Every Christian who does not make prayer a mighty factor in his own life and ministry is weak as a factor in God's work and powerless to project

God's cause in this world.

Prayer is the Christian's mightiest weapon. An almighty force in itself, it gives life and force to all.

Questions for Personal Insight and Group Discussion

Part 1: System vs. Spirit

1. What kinds of "new methods" does the church today rely on to advance the gospel of Jesus Christ?

2. Why are people more important than programs in God's system? Who are some of the people who have influenced my life for Christ?

3. Why does God choose to use people to spread his Word? What are the advantages and disadvantages of this plan?

4. How have I influenced someone else for Christ? How can I, as an individual, participate in the advancement of God's kingdom?

Part 2: Character

1. Why does Bounds say that a Christian's character has more to do with spreading the gospel than preaching does?

2. How does an individual's inner life affect the outward ministry, both for good and for evil?

3. If character determines the message, what is "my gospel"—the message my life communicates?

4.   How can I change my life to make it, and its resulting message, conform more closely to the image of Christ?

Part 3: Living Words

1.   When Bounds speaks of "dead words," how does that apply to situations other than preaching?

2.   What does holiness mean? How does it apply to the modern believer? What does a "saint" look like?

3.   What does it mean to "impersonate the gospel"? How can I do that in my daily life?

4.   Bounds says that the believer must be "hearty, heroic, compassionate, fearless." What specific situations in my everyday life call for heroism or fearlessness?

Part 4: Preparing Ourselves Through Prayer

1.   Why is preparing myself of utmost importance if I wish to serve God? How do I do it?

2.   Bounds says that holiness, faith, and fidelity are more important to God's purposes than natural ability. How is this an encouragement to the "ordinary" Christian?

3.   What does Bounds mean when he says, "Real ministry is made in the closet"? How does my life become "real ministry" to those around me?

4.   What strengths other than prayer, the power of the Spirit, and the grace of God do I tend to depend upon? What does "the dependent humility of prayer" mean to me in my own Christian life?

2

Our Sufficiency Is of God

But above all he excelled in prayer. . . . He knew and lived nearer to the Lord than other men, for they that know him most will see most reason to approach him with reverence and fear.

—William Penn, speaking of George Fox

Two Sides of the Coin

The sweetest graces by a slight perversion may bear the bitterest fruit. The sun gives life, but sunstrokes are death. Words give life; they may also kill. The believer holds the keys; he may lock as well as unlock. Speaking the word is God's great institution for planting and maturing spiritual life. When properly executed, its benefits are untold; when wrongly executed, no evil can exceed its damaging results.

It is an easy matter to destroy the flock if the shepherd is unwary or the pasture destroyed; it is easy to capture the citadel if the watchmen are asleep or the food and water poisoned.

The ministry of Christ is invested with gracious prerogatives, exposed to great evils, subject to grave responsibilities. The Devil brings his masterful influences to adulterate the minister and the ministry. Paul's exclamation, "Who is sufficient for these things?" (2 Corinthians 2:16) applies today.

The Spirit-touched Life

Paul continues: "Our sufficiency is of God; Who also hath made us able ministers of the new testament; not of the letter, but of the spirit: for the letter killeth, but the spirit giveth life" (2 Corinthians 3:5-6). True ministry is God-touched, God-enabled, and God-made. The Spirit of God is on his people in anointing power; the fruit of the Spirit is in their hearts.

The Spirit of God vitalizes the believer and the word; the word gives life as the spring gives life, gives life as the resurrection gives life. The word gives ardent life as the summer gives ardent life; it gives fruitful life as the autumn gives fruitful life.

The life-giving Christian is a man or woman of God, whose heart is ever athirst for God, whose soul is ever following hard after God, and in whom by the power of God's Spirit the flesh and the world have been crucified. Such ministry is like the generous flood of a life-giving river.

The Word That Kills

The word that kills is a nonspiritual word. The ability to speak eloquently is not necessarily from God. Lower sources than God can give it energy and stimulant, but the Spirit is not evident in the minister or the ministry. Many kinds of forces may be projected and stimulated by words that kill, but they are not spiritual forces. They may resemble spiritual forces, but they are only the shadow, the counterfeit.

The word that kills is the letter of the law. Shapely and orderly it may be, but it is the letter still, the dry, husky letter, the empty, bald shell. The letter of the law may have the term of life in it, but it has no breath of spring to evoke it. They are winter seeds, as hard as the winter's soil, as icy as the winter's air; there is no thawing or germinating by them.

This letter-preaching contains the truth. But even divine truth has no life-giving energy alone; it must be energized by the Spirit, with all God's forces at its back. Truth unquickened by God's Spirit deadens as much as, or more than, error. It may be the truth, pure and untainted, but without the Spirit its shade and touch are deadly, its truth error, its light darkness.

Pretense and Powerlessness

The word that kills is powerless, unanointed by the Holy Spirit. There may be tears, but tears cannot fuel the machinery of God's kingdom. Tears may be only summer's breath on a snow-covered iceberg—nothing but surface slush. Feelings and earnestness may be mere pretense—the emotions of the actor and the earnestness of the attorney.

Proclaimers of the word of death may warm to the kindling of their own sparks, be eloquent over their own exegesis, earnest in delivering the products of their own brains. The professor may usurp the place and imitate the fire of the apostle; brains and nerves may serve the place and feign the work of God's Spirit. By these forces the letter of the law may glow and sparkle like an illuminated text. But the glow and sparkle will be as barren of life as the field sown with pearls.

The death-dealing element lies back of the words, back of the sermon, back of the occasion, back of the manner, back of the action. The great hindrance is in the speakers themselves. They do have in themselves the mighty life-creating forces. There may be no fault in their orthodoxy, honesty, cleanness, or earnestness. But somehow the inner person in its secret places has never broken down and surrendered to God; the inner life is not a great highway for the transmission of God's message, God's power. Somehow self and not God rules in the holy of holies.

Somewhere, unconsciously, some spiritual nonconductor has touched the inner being, and the divine current has been arrested. The inner person has never felt its thorough spiritual bankruptcy, its utter powerlessness. The speaker has never learned to cry out with an ineffable cry of self-despair and self-helplessness till God's power and God's fire comes in and fills, purifies, empowers. Self-esteem, self-ability in some pernicious shape has defamed and violated the temple which should be held sacred for God.

Life-giving ministry costs the minister much—death to self, crucifixion to the world, the travail of the soul. Crucified ministry only can give life, and crucified ministry can only come from a crucified soul.

Questions for Personal Insight and Group Discussion

Part 1: Two Sides of the Coin

1.   What does Bounds mean when he says, "Words give life; they may also kill"?

2.   What kind of death comes from the spoken word? What kind of life?

3.   What are the responsibilities of the person who ministers God's word?

4.   How does the Enemy attempt to undermine godly ministry?

Part 2: The Spirit-touched Life

1.   What does "the anointing of the Spirit" mean? How do I know when someone (myself or another) is speaking an "anointed" word?

2.   How does the word give life? What are the results?

3.   What is the difference between the "letter" of God's Word and the "spirit"?

4.   As long as I am speaking the truth and being true to the written Word of God, what difference does it make whether my personal life conforms to God's standards, or whether I truly seek him with all my heart?

Part 3: The Word That Kills

1.   When the words sound good and the techniques of delivery are flawless, how do I know when a speaker is speaking a "nonspiritual" message?

2.   What does Bounds mean when he says, "The word that kills is the letter of the law"? Why is the "letter" empty of life and power?

3.   Bounds says, "Truth unquickened by God's Spirit deadens as much as, or more than, error." What does he mean?

4.   When have I heard someone speak "dead words"? What was my response?

Part 4: Pretense and Powerlessness

1.   What is the difference between emotion and anointing?

2.   Why are some speakers able to generate a great deal of emotion without the anointing of the Holy Spirit?

3.   What is the underlying source of the "death" in a person who ministers apart from the empowering of God's Spirit?

4.   Why are powerlessness, helplessness, and death to self essential prerequisites for a life-giving ministry?

3

The Letter Kills

During this affliction I was brought to examine my life in relation to eternity. . . . [As] a Christian minister, and an officer of the church, I stood approved by my own conscience; but in relation to my Redeemer and Saviour the result was different. . . . [I had] declined from first zeal and love. I was confounded, humbled myself, implored mercy, and renewed my covenant to strive and devote myself unreservedly to the Lord.

—Bishop McKendree

Orthodoxy

The word that kills may be, and often is, orthodox—dogmatically, inviolably orthodox. We love orthodoxy. It is the clean, clear-cut teaching of God's Word, the trophies won by truth in its conflict with error, the levees which faith has raised against the desolating floods of honest or reckless misbelief or unbelief.

But orthodoxy, clear and hard as crystal, suspicious and militant, may be but the law well-shaped, well-named, and well-learned—the letter of the law which kills. Nothing is so dead as dead orthodoxy, too dead to speculate, too dead to think, to study, or to pray.

The word that kills may have insight and grasp of principles; it may be scholarly and critical; it may be perfect in grammar and expression. One may study the word as a lawyer studies textbooks, to form a brief or defend a case, and yet it is like a frost, a killing frost. The word that kills may be eloquent, enameled with poetry and rhetoric, sprinkled with prayer, spiced with sensation, illuminated by genius. But these are only the costly mountings, the rare and beautiful flowers, which coffin the corpse.

The word that kills may also be without scholarship, unmarked by any freshness of thought or feeling, reflecting neither meditation nor study, graced neither by thought, expression, nor prayer. In either case, it leaves utter desolation, profound spiritual death, in its wake.

The Shadow

This letter of the law deals with the surface and shadow of things; it does not penetrate the inner part. It has no deep insight into, no strong grasp of, the hidden life of God's Word. It is true to the outside, but the outside is the hull which must be broken and penetrated for the kernel. The word may be dressed so as to be attractive and fashionable, but the attraction is not toward God, nor is the fashion for heaven.

The failure is in the ones who minister these dead words. They have never been in the hands of God like clay in the hands of the potter. They have been busy about building the ministry, making it attractive and impressive; but they have never sought, studied, fathomed, experienced the deep things of God. They have never stood before the "throne, high and lifted up," (Isaiah 6:1) never heard the seraphim song, never seen the vision nor felt the rush of that awful holiness. They have never cried out in utter abandon and despair under the sense of weakness and guilt, and had their lives renewed, their hearts touched, purged, inflamed by the live coal from God's altar.

Such ministry may draw people to the speaker, to the church, to the form and ceremony, but not to God; no sweet, divine communion is induced. The church has been frescoed but not edified, pleased but not sanctified. Life is suppressed; a chill is on the summer air; the soil is baked. The city of our God becomes the city of the dead; the church a graveyard, not an embattled army. Praise and prayer are stifled; worship dies. The ministry of the letter has helped sin, not holiness; populated hell, not heaven.

Prayer and Power

Ministry which kills is prayerless ministry. Without prayer we create death, and not life. If we are feeble in prayer, we are feeble in life-giving forces. If we have retired prayer as a conspicuous and largely prevailing element in our own characters, we have shorn the word of its distinctive life-giving power.

Professional praying in the worship service will always exist, but professional praying helps the dead word do its deadly work. Professional praying chills and kills both the word and true prayer. Much of the lax devotion and lazy, irreverent attitudes in congregational praying are attributable to professional praying in the pulpit.

Long, discursive, dry, and inane are the prayers in many pulpits. Without anointing or heart, they fall like a killing frost on the graces of worship. Death-dealing prayers they are. Every vestige of devotion has perished under their breath. The deader they are the longer they grow. In the pulpit, we need short praying, live praying, real heart praying, praying by the Holy Spirit—direct, specific, simple, ardent.

Are we ministering to kill, or to give life? Are we praying to kill, or to give life? We are praying to God, the great God, the Maker of all worlds, the Judge of all men! What reverence, what simplicity, what sincerity, what inner truth is demanded when we approach him! Prayer to God is the noblest exercise, the loftiest effort of the human soul. We must discard forever the word that kills and prayer that kills, and do the mightiest thing— prayerful praying, life-creating ministry. We must bring the mightiest force to bear on heaven and earth and draw on God's inexhaustible treasure for the needs of those we serve.

Questions for Personal Insight and Group Discussion

Part 1: Orthodoxy

1. What does Bounds mean by "orthodoxy"? Why does orthodoxy fail to communicate spiritual life?

2. Paul says, "My speech and my preaching was not with enticing words of man's wisdom, but in demonstration of the Spirit and of power: That your faith should not stand in the wisdom of men, but in the power of God" (1 Corinthians 2:4-5). Why is eloquence not the main criterion for life-giving ministry? What is the basis for the word that brings life?

3. Have I ever heard a speaker whose words and delivery were flawless, yet there seemed to be "something missing"? What was missing? What was my response?

4. Why is it easier to speak well than to minister life?

Part 2: The Shadow

1. How can a speaker be faithful to the surface truth of the word and yet fail to communicate life?

2. What is the difference between "building a ministry" and "being in the hands of God"?

3. Why is abandoning myself to God essential if I want to speak the words of life to others? What happens when I give myself into God's hands?

4. What does Bounds mean when he says, "The church has been frescoed but not edified"? In what ways can the church be decorated and yet devoid of life?

Part 3: Prayer and Power

1. Is "professional praying" wrong? Why or why not? How can professional praying be a hindrance to true spiritual life?

2. What is "live prayer"? What examples of live prayer and dead prayer have I seen in my own life?

3. When I truly perceive the glory and greatness of God, how will my prayer life change?

4. Why is prayer to God "the noblest exercise, the loftiest effort of the human soul"? Has that been my experience in prayer?

4

The Pre-eminence of
Prayer

*Prayer—secret, fervent, believing prayer—lies at the root of all
personal godliness.*

—Carrey's Brotherhood, Serampore

Two Extremes

Two extreme tendencies arise in ministry. One is to shut
out interaction with the people. The monk and the
hermit shut themselves out from others to be more with
God. They failed, of course. Being with God is of use
only as we expend its priceless benefits on others.

But this age is not much intent on God. We shut
ourselves in to our studies; we become students, book-
worms, Bible worms, sermon makers, noted for literature, thought, and expression. But the people of God are
out of heart, out of mind. Great thinkers and great
students must be the greatest of prayers, or else they will

be the greatest of backsliders, heartless professionals, rationalistic, not true ministers in God's estimate.

The other tendency is thoroughly to popularize the ministry. We no longer are God's servants, but people of affairs. Thus we do not pray, because our mission is to the people. If we can move the people, create an interest, a sensation in favor of religion, an interest in church work, we are satisfied. Our personal relation to God is no factor in our work. Prayer has little or no place in our plans.

The disaster and ruin of such a ministry cannot be computed. Our power in prayer to God, for ourselves and for the people we serve, is our power for real good to others. Prayer determines our true fruitfulness to God and man, for time and eternity.

The Effect of Prayer

It is impossible for us to keep our spirits in harmony with the divine nature of our high calling without much prayer. If we believe that by dint of duty and laborious fidelity to the work and routine of the ministry we can keep ourselves spiritually fit, we have made a serious mistake. All ministry will engross and harden, will estrange the heart from God, by neglect of prayer.

Prayer freshens our hearts, keeps us in tune with God and in sympathy with the people, lifts our ministry out of the chilly air of professionalism, makes routine fruitful, and moves every wheel with the facility and power of divine enabling.

Mr. Spurgeon says: "All our libraries and studies are mere emptiness compared with our closets (i.e., the prayer closet). Our seasons of fasting and prayer at the Tabernacle have been high days indeed; never has heaven's gate stood wider; never have our hearts been nearer the central Glory."

The Pre-eminence of Prayer

Prayer which makes a powerful ministry is not put in as we put in flavor, to give it a pleasant smack. True praying must be in the body, and form the blood and bones. Prayer is no petty duty, put into a corner; no piecemeal performance made out of fragments of time snatched from business and other engagements of life. True prayer must be the best of our time, the heart of our time and strength. The closet of prayer must not be absorbed in the study or swallowed up in activity. When prayer comes first, both study and activities are energized and enlivened.

Prayer that affects our ministry must first give depth to our private lives. The praying which directs the development of character is no pleasant, hurried pastime. It must enter as strongly into the heart and life as Christ's "strong crying and tears"* did. It must draw out the soul into an agony of desire as Paul's did.** It must be an inwrought fire and force like the "effectual fervent prayer" (James 5:16) of James. When put into the

---

* Bounds's quotation is not a specific scriptural reference. Examples of Jesus' intensity in prayer, however, are found in the Gospel accounts of his prayers in the Garden of Gethsemane: Matthew 26:36ff; Mark 14:32ff; and Luke 22:39ff. A similar depth of commitment in prayer seems to be indicated in other places, such as the raising of Lazarus (John 11) and the Lord's lament over the unfaithfulness of Jersalem (Matthew 23:37-39; Luke 13:34-35).

** In Romans 9:2-3, Paul says, "I have great heaviness and continual sorrow in my heart. For I could wish that myself were accursed from Christ for my brethren, my kinsmen according to the flesh."

golden censer and offered up to God, true prayer works mighty spiritual changes.

Prayer is not a little habit pinned on to us while we were tied to our mothers' apron strings; neither is it a quarter of a minute's grace said over an hour's dinner. Prayer is a most serious work of our most serious years. It engages more time and appetite than our longest, richest feasts.

The character of our praying will determine the character of our ministries. Prayer makes our words strong, gives them power, makes them stick. In every anointed ministry, prayer has always been a serious business.

We must be pre-eminently people of prayer. Our hearts must graduate in the school of prayer, for only in the school of prayer can the heart learn to minister. No learning can make up for the failure to pray. No earnestness, no diligence, no study will supply its lack.

Talking to others for God is a great thing. But talking to God for others is greater still. We will never speak to people for God with real success until we have learned how to speak to God for people.

Questions for Personal Insight and Group Discussion

Part 1: Two Extremes

1. Why does Bounds say that the monks and hermits failed in their attempts to be closer to God?

2. Why is the life of the hermit an attractive one to some believers? In what ways does it offer fellowship with God? In what ways does it present hindrances to a closer relationship with him?

3. What does it mean to "popularize the ministry"? What examples of "popular ministry" have I seen? Why is this tendency dangerous to spiritual life?

4. What happens when a Christian perceives of a ministry as a "job" rather than a "calling"?

Part 2: The Effect of Prayer

1. Bounds says that prayerless ministry will "engross and harden, will estrange the heart from God." We often call this effect "burnout." Why does lack of prayer contribute to burnout?

2. Have I ever felt burned out, estranged from God? Why? How can I be restored after burnout?

3. Why does prayer bring me nearer to the "central Glory" of God than study?

Part 3: The Pre-eminence of Prayer

1. How do I perceive my own prayer life? Is it "blood and bones" of my spiritual experience, or "piecemeal performance"?

2.   Why do we have such a tendency to let prayer become a minor activity, an add-on to the Christian life?

3.   What do the biblical examples of Jesus, Paul, and James teach me about the importance of prayer?

4.   How does the character of my praying determine the character of my ministry to others?

5

The Essential Nature of Prayer

You know the value of prayer: it is precious beyond all price. Never, never neglect it.

—Sir Thomas Buxton

Power and the Person

Prayer, in the Christian's life, in the Christian's study, in the Christian's ministry, must be a conspicuous and all-encompassing force. It must play no secondary part. We need to be with our Lord "all night in prayer" (Luke 6:12). To train ourselves in self-denying prayer, we must look to the Master: "Rising up a great while before day, he went out, and departed into a solitary place, and there prayed" (Mark 1:35). We need a Bethel, an altar, a vision, and a ladder,* that every thought might ascend

---

* "Bethel" means "House of God." The first scriptural reference to Beth--el is found in Genesis 12:8. Abram pitched his tent east of Beth-el and

heavenward, that every word might be scented by the air of heaven and made serious, because God was present in our praying.

As a steam engine never moves until the fire is kindled, so ministry, with all its perfection and polish, remains at a standstill, as far as spiritual results are concerned, until prayer has kindled the fire and created the steam. The texture, fineness, and strength of our speaking is rubbish unless the mighty impulse of prayer is in it, through it, and behind it. We must, by prayer, put God in our words. We must, by prayer, move God toward the people before we can move the people to God by our words. We must have ready access to God before we can have access to others. An open way to God is the surest pledge of an open way to the people.

True Prayer

Prayer as a mere habit, a performance, or a routine, is a dead and rotten thing. True praying engages and sets on fire every high element of the Christian's being. Prayer is born out of vital oneness with Christ and the fullness of the Holy Ghost. It springs from the deep, overflowing fountains of tender compassion and concern for humanity's eternal good. True prayer is a consuming zeal for the glory of God; it involves a

---

there "builded an altar unto the Lord, and called upon the name of the Lord." In Genesis 28, Beth-el, then called Luz, was the location of Jacob's famous dream. In the dream, Jacob saw heaven opened and a ladder extending down toward earth. He heard the voice of God, and when he arose, he said, "This is none other but the house of God, and this is the gate of heaven" (Genesis 28:17). And he set up an altar and named the place Beth-el.

thorough conviction of the difficult and delicate work of the ministry and the imperative need of God's help. Praying grounded on these solemn and profound convictions is the only true praying. And only ministry backed by such praying sows the seeds of eternal life in human hearts and builds others up for heaven.

Ministry today may be popular, pleasant, attractive, intellectual, intriguing, and successful with little or no prayer. But the ministry which accomplishes God's purposes must be born of prayer from beginning to end.

Spiritual Work

We may excuse our spiritual poverty in many ways, but the reason will be found in the lack of urgent prayer for God's presence in the power of the Spirit. A speaker can deliver a masterful sermon, but the effects are short-lived and superficial. In the regions of the spirit, a fearful war rages between God and Satan, heaven and hell; we are only spiritually victorious through prayer.

Christians who gain lasting results for God are those who have prevailed in their pleadings with God before venturing to plead with others. Those who are mightiest in their closets with God are mightiest in their efforts with men and women.

Christians are human, and are exposed to and often caught by the strong driftings of human currents. Praying is spiritual work, and human nature does not like taxing, spiritual work. Human nature wants to sail to heaven under a favorable breeze on a full, smooth sea. Prayer is humbling work, abasing the intellect and pride, crucifying self, admitting spiritual bankruptcy. Such humbling is hard for flesh and blood to bear; we would rather not pray than bear them.

And so we resort to little or no praying. Of these two evils, perhaps little praying is worse than no praying. Little praying is a kind of make-believe, a salve for the conscience, a farce, and a delusion.

The Time Factor

The little estimate we put on prayer is evident from the little time we give to it. The time given to prayer by the average Christian scarcely counts in the sum of daily activities. Often our only praying is by our bedside—or in our beds—before we fall asleep, or brief snatches of prayer as we dress for the day. How feeble, vain, and little is such praying compared with the time and energy devoted to praying by holy men and women in and out of the Bible! Our petty and childish praying is shamed by the habits of the true men and women of God in all ages.

To those who think praying is their main business and devote time to it according to this high estimate of its importance, God commits the keys of his kingdom, and by them he works his spiritual wonders in this world. Great praying is the sign and seal of God's great leaders.

We are commissioned to pray as well as to speak the word. This mission is incomplete if we do not do both well. We may speak with all the eloquence of angels; but unless we can pray with a faith which draws all heaven to our aid, our words will be "as sounding brass, or a tinkling cymbal" (1 Corinthians 13:1) for permanent, God-honoring, soul-saving uses.

Questions for Personal Insight and Group Discussion

Part 1: Power and the Person

1. Bounds speaks of prayer as a "Bethel," the place where God dwells. What "Bethel" experiences have I had in my own prayer life?

2. What is Jesus' example of prayer? Is the specific time of day important? Why or why not?

3. How does prayer kindle the fire and create the steam in ministry?

4. Have I ever tried to minister to someone without the kindling fire of prayer? What was the result?

Part 2: True Prayer

1. According to Bounds, prayer is "born out of vital oneness with Christ." Why is love for Christ the primary motive for prayer? What other motives can I identify? What is the difference between prayer motivated by love and prayer motivated by some other reason?

2. Why is ministry a "difficult and delicate work"?

3. What are some of the signs of a prayerless ministry?

4. What are the signs of a prayer-filled ministry?

Part 3: Spiritual Work

1. What does it mean to "prevail in our pleading with God"?

2. What are some of the "driftings of human currents" to

which the Christian is subject? How do these forces affect my spiritual life?

3. How does prayer help me to stand firm against those currents?

4. Why does Bounds say that little praying is worse than not praying at all?

Part 4: The Time Factor

1. How much time to I spend each day in prayer. Does my prayer life fall into Bounds's category of "little praying"?

2. What specific examples does the Bible provide of people who prayed mightily?

3. How can I emulate the examples of great biblical prayers? What aspects of their prayer habits apply to me? Which do not necessarily apply?

4. Bounds describes true prayer as praying "with a faith which draws all heaven to our aid." Have I ever experienced this kind of power in prayer? Is this description an encouragement or a frustration to me? Why?

6

Successful
Praying

*Prayer and patience and faith are never disappointed. I have
long since learned that if ever I was to be a minister faith and
prayer must make me one.*

—Richard Newton

The Controlling Force

In every truly successful ministry prayer is an evident
and controlling force—evident and controlling in the
life of the believer, evident and controlling in the deep
spirituality of the work. A ministry may be a very
thoughtful ministry without prayer; we may secure
fame and popularity without prayer; our lives may be
run without the oil of prayer or with scarcely enough to
grease a single cog. But no ministry can be a spiritual
one, resulting in holiness, without prayer as an evident
and controlling force.

When we pray, we put God into the work. God does
not involve himself in our activity as a matter of course

or on general principle; he comes by prayer. God will be found of us in the day that we seek him with our whole heart (Jeremiah 29:13).

Just as prayer brings us into union with God, a prayerful ministry brings us into sympathy with the people we serve. Prayer unites human to human as it does human to divine. The high responsibilities of ministry to others demands a high level of commitment to prayer.

Holiness

Colleges, learning, books, theology cannot make a minister, but praying does. The apostles' commission to preach was a blank until filled up by the Spirit at Pentecost; they prayed until the Spirit empowered.* As prayerful Christians, we pass beyond the regions of the popular into a more sublime and mightier region, the region of the spiritual. Holiness is the product of this work; transfigured hearts and lives emblazon the reality of this work, its trueness and substantial nature. God is with us.

The ministry marked by prayer is not projected on worldly or surface principles. People of holiness are deeply schooled in the things of God. Their com-

---

*Bounds's reference is a composite of scriptural accounts. Matthew 28:18-20 gives the "Great Commission" of Christ to his disciples—they were commanded to teach all nations and baptize. Luke 24:49 records Christ's promise of the coming Holy Spirit and his instructions to "tarry ye in the city of Jerusalem, until ye be endued with power from on high." Acts 1 repeats these last words of Jesus and chronicles his ascension into heaven, and Acts 2 shows the fulfillment of both the promise and the command—the believers are filled with the Holy Spirit and begin to preach the Word.

munings with God about his people, their wrestling in prayer with him, crown them with a diadem of righteousness. The iciness of mere profession melts under the intensity of such praying.

The superficial results of many a ministry, and the deadness of others, are to be found in the lack of praying. No ministry can succeed without much prayer, and this prayer must be fundamental, constant, ever-increasing. The spoken word and the example of the Christian's life should be the result of prayer. Bible study should be bathed in prayer, and all the Christian's efforts made fruitful by prayer. "I am sorry that I have prayed so little," was the deathbed regret of one of God's chosen ones, a sad and remorseful regret for a minister of the gospel. The late Archbishop Tait said, "I want a life of greater, deeper, truer prayer." The longing of his heart is a model for all who wish to draw closer to the Lord.

The Center Attraction

God's true saints have been distinguished by one outstanding feature: they were all people of prayer. Differing often in many points, they have always had a common center. They may have started from different places and traveled by different roads, but they converged upon one crossroad: they were one in prayer. God to them was the center attraction, and prayer was the path that led to God.

These men and women did not pray occasionally, a little at regular or at odd times; they prayed so that their prayers entered into and shaped their characters. They prayed so as to affect their own lives and the lives of others; they prayed so as to direct the history of the church and to influence the current of their times. They spent much time in prayer, not because they marked the shadow on the dial or the hands on the clock, but because it was to them such a momentous and engaging business that they could scarcely give it up.

Prayer was to these saints what it was to Paul, striving with earnest effort of soul (Romans 15:30). Like Jacob, they wrestled and prevailed (Genesis 32:24-28); like Christ, they gave themselves over to "strong crying and tears."* They prayed "always with all prayer and supplication in the Spirit, and watching thereunto with all perseverance" (Ephesians 6:18).

"Effectual fervent prayer" (James 5:16) has always been the mightiest weapon of God's most valiant soldiers. Elijah "was a man subject to like passions as we are, and he prayed earnestly that it might not rain: and it rained not on the earth by the space of three years and six months. And he prayed again, and the heaven gave rain, and the earth brought forth her fruit" (James 5:17-18). His example applies to all prophets who have moved their generation for God. Prayer is the instrument by which they worked their wonders.

*See chapter 4, first note.

Questions for Personal Insight and Group Discussion

Part 1: The Controlling Force

1. How is prayer an "evident and controlling force" in the believer's life? Is it such a force in my life? Why or why not?

2. How can I pray effectively for God's Spirit to be at work in my ministry to others?

3. How does prayer unite me with God?

4. How does prayer unite me with others?

Part 2: Holiness

1. The disciples were commissioned to "go into the world" and then commanded to "wait in Jerusalem" until the Holy Spirit came upon them. Why is waiting for the Holy Spirit's empowering essential also to my calling in Christ?

2. What does "holiness" mean to me in my present life circumstances? How can I seek holiness in my life, and what changes might I expect to see as I draw closer to God?

3. How does personal holiness affect the result of my life's example and the words I speak?

4. Do I desire a life of "deeper, truer prayer"? How can I attain that desire?

Part 3: The Center Attraction

1. What is the common definition of "saint"? The biblical definition? What individuals living in this generation are regarded as "saints"?

2.   If God is the "center attraction" in my life, what will be the result in my outward behavior?

3.   What is my concept of "effectual fervent prayer"? How can I make such prayer central in my life?

4.   Was the prophet Elijah different from anyone else? What made his prayers so effective?

7

Mastering
Time With God

*The act of praying is the very highest energy of which the
human mind is capable; praying, that is, with the total concentration of the faculties. The great mass of worldly men and of
learned men are absolutely incapable of prayer.*

—Samuel Taylor Coleridge

Giving Time

Many private prayers, in the nature of things, must be
short; public prayers, as a rule, ought to be short and
condensed. Yet in our private communion with God,
time is essential to its value. Much time spent with God
is the secret of all successful praying. Prayer which is felt
as a mighty force is the product of time with God.

Our short prayers owe their point and efficiency to
the long ones that have preceded them. The short
prevailing prayer cannot be prayed by one who has not
struggled with God in long continuance. Jacob's victory
of faith could not have been gained without that all-

night wrestling (Genesis 32:24).

God does not bestow his gifts on the casual or hasty comers and goers. He yields to the persistency of a faith that knows him. He bestows his richest treasures on those who declare their desire for and appreciation of those gifts by the constancy and earnestness of their prayers.

Christ, who in this and many other principles is our example, spent many whole nights in prayer (Luke 6:12). His custom was to pray often, and he had his habitual places of prayer. Many long seasons of praying make up our Lord's history and character. In the midst of life-threatening circumstances, Daniel took the time to pray three times a day (Daniel 6:10). Similarly, David's morning, noon, and night prayers (Psalm 55:17) were no doubt often protracted. While we have no specific account of the time these Bible saints spent in prayer, yet the Scripture indicates that they consumed much time in prayer, and that often long seasons of praying was their custom.

The value of our prayers is not, of course, measured by the clock; long lifeless prayers are of no more value than short lifeless ones. But we need time to be alone with God; if this practice has not been produced by our faith, then our faith is merely a surface shell, void of reality.

Examples of Prayer

The men and women who have most fully illustrated Christ in their character, and have most powerfully affected the world for him, have been people who spent so much time with God as to make it a notable feature of their lives. Wesley spent two hours daily in prayer, beginning at four in the morning. "He thought prayer to be more his business than anything else." John Fletcher would sometimes pray all night; he always prayed frequently, and with great earnestness. His greeting to his friends was always, "Do I meet you praying?"

Luther said, "If I fail to spend two hours in prayer each morning, the Devil gets the victory through the day. I have so much business I cannot get on without spending three hours daily in prayer." Luther's motto was, "He that has prayed well has studied well."

Others give us examples of commitment to prayer as well. Joseph Alleine arose at four o'clock for his business of praying. If he heard other tradesmen at work before he was up, he would exclaim, "O, how this shames me! Doth not my Master deserve more than theirs?"

One of the holiest and most gifted of Scottish preachers, Robert McCheyne, says, "I ought to spend the best hours in communion with God. It is my noblest and most fruitful employment, and is not to be thrust into a corner."

Prayer and Work

The Marquis DeRenty, to whom Christ was most precious, ordered his servant to call him from his devotions at the end of half an hour. The servant came at the appointed time and saw his master's face, marked with such holiness that he hated to interrupt him. His lips were moving, but he was perfectly silent. After an hour and a half had passed, the servant reluctantly called his master. DeRenty arose from his knees, saying that half an hour was all too short when he was communing with Christ.

Dr. Judson's success in ministry is attributable to the fact that he gave much time to prayer:

> Arrange thy affairs, if possible, so that thou canst leisurely devote two or three hours every day not merely to devotional exercises but to the very act of secret prayer and communion with God. Endeavor seven times a day to withdraw from business and company and lift up thy soul to God in private retirement. Begin the day by rising after midnight and devoting some time amid the silence and darkness of the night to this sacred work. Let the hour of opening dawn find thee at the same work. . . . Consider that thy time is short, and that business and company must not be allowed to rob thee of thy God.

We read these words and think, "Impossible! Fanatical!" Yet Dr. Judson impressed an empire for Christ and laid the foundations of God's kingdom in the heart of Burma. He was successful, one of the few men who mightily impressed the world for Christ. Many men of greater gifts and genius and learning than he have made no such impression. Their religious work is like footsteps in the sand, but he chiseled his work in the Rock.

The secret of the profundity and endurance of Judson's work is found in the fact that he gave time to prayer. He kept the iron red-hot with prayer, and God's skill fashioned it with enduring power. No one can do a great and enduring work for God who is not a man or woman of prayer; and no one can be a person of prayer who does not give much time to praying.

Questions for Personal Insight and Group Discussion

Part 1: Giving Time

1. Why does Bounds indicate that the effectiveness of short prayers depends upon the long ones that have preceded them?

2. Bounds says, "God does not bestow his gifts on the casual or hasty comers and goers." Why does God reserve his deepest treasures for those who devote time to him?

3. Are God's blessings simply a reward for those who work for them, spending long hours with him? Why does commitment to prayer result in knowledge of God?

4. If time itself is not the measure of effective prayer, why is it important to spend extended time with God in prayer?

Part 2: Examples of Prayer

1. Bounds records a number of examples of people who prayed mightily. All of them rose quite early to spend several hours in prayer. Is this practice necessary? Why or why not?

2. How would I respond to John Fletcher's question, "Do I meet you praying?"

3. Often we say that "quality is more important than quantity." How does this statement apply to my prayer life? Is it a rationalization for prayerlessness?

4. What is my response to the examples of prayer Bounds provides? How do these examples apply to my life?

Part 3: Prayer and Work

1. The Marquis DeRenty, according to Bounds's account, completely lost track of time when he was in the presence of the Lord. Have I ever had that experience? When, and under what circumstances?

2. Are these examples of holiness and devotion merely relics from another era, or do their lives and practices apply to Christians today?

3. Is it possible for me to devote the kind of time to prayer recommended by Judson? Is it practical? Is it necessary?

4. Does the depth of my prayer life depend upon the particular type of calling I have from God? (i.e., does a "professional" in Christian ministry—a pastor, counselor, teacher, etc.—have a higher expectation in prayer?) What does it depend on?

8

Beginning the Day With Prayer

I ought to pray before seeing any one. . . . It is far better to begin with God—to see his face first, to get my soul near him before it is near another.

—Robert Murray McCheyne

Seeking God Early

The men and women who have done the most for God in this world have been early on their knees. When we fritter away the early morning's opportunities and freshness in pursuits other than seeking God, we will make poor headway seeking him the rest of the day. If God is not first in our thoughts and efforts in the morning, he will be in the last place in the evening.

The motive behind this early rising and early praying is an ardent desire to pursue God. Morning listlessness indicates a listless heart; the heart which is slow in seeking God in the morning has lost its relish for God.

David's heart was ardent after God. He hungered and thirsted after God, and so sought God early, before daylight (Psalms 57:8; 63:1; 108:2; 119:147). The comforts of bed and sleep could not chain his soul in its eagerness for God's presence.

Christ longed for communion with God; rising before daybreak, he would go out into the mountain to pray (Mark 1:35; Luke 6:12-13). Later his disciples, fully awake and ashamed of their indulgences, knew where to find him.

A desire for God which cannot break the chains of sleep is weak, able to do little for God after it has indulged itself fully. The desire for God that lags behind the Devil and the world at the beginning of the day will never catch up.

Desiring God

It is not simply getting up that puts great men and women of God to the front and makes them generals in God's army. It is, rather, the ardent desire which stirs and breaks all self-indulgent chains. Getting up gives vent, increase, and strength to the desire. If we lay in bed and indulge ourselves, the desire is quenched.

The desire for God awoke the great saints of God and called them to communion with their Lord. Heeding and acting on this call gave their faith its grasp on God and gave to their hearts the sweetest and fullest revelation of God. Strength of faith and fullness of revelation made them saints by eminence; the halo of their sainthood has come down to us, and we enjoy their conquests. But we are satisfied with enjoyment, not with production. We build their tombs and write their epitaphs, but we do not follow their examples.

We need a generation of believers who seek God and seek him early, who give the freshness and dew of effort to God, and secure in return the freshness and fullness of his power. He is the early dew, full of gladness and strength, that refreshes us through the heat and labor of the day.

The children of this world are far wiser than we; they work early and late. We do not seek God with such ardor and diligence. No one approaches God who does not follow hard after him, and no soul follows hard after God who is not after him in early morn.

Questions for Personal Insight and Group Discussion

Part 1: Seeking God Early

1. Bounds says, "If God is not first in our thoughts and efforts in the morning, he will be in last place the remainder of the day." Is he right? What experiences have I had that either support or negate the statement?

2. How does my day usually begin? Am I conscious of the presence of God from the beginning?

3. How does the beginning of the day set the tone and give direction for the rest of the day? Give examples.

Part 2: Desiring God

1. What does Bounds mean when he says that getting up gives strength to the desire for God? How have I experienced that truth?

2. Concerning the saints who have gone before, Bounds says, "We build their tombs and write their epitaphs, but do not follow their examples." What does he mean?

3. Do I "follow hard after God"? What does that mean in my own spiritual experience?

9

Prayer and Devotion

The ministry is a grand and holy affair, and it should find in us a simple habit of spirit and a holy but humble indifference to all consequences. The leading defect in Christian ministers is want of a devotional habit.

—Richard Cecil

The Fullness of Christ

Never was there greater need for saintly men and women, for God-devoted ministers. The world moves with gigantic strides. Satan has his hold and rule on the world, and labors to make all its movements serve his ends. Religion must do its best work, present its most attractive and perfect models. By every means, modern sainthood must be inspired by the loftiest ideals and by the largest possibilities through the Spirit.

Paul lived on his knees, that the Ephesian church might measure the heights, breadths, and depths of an unmeasurable saintliness, and "be filled with all the fulness of God" (Ephesians 3:14-19). Epaphras laid himself out with the exhaustive toil and strenuous conflict of fervent prayer that the Colossian church might "stand perfect and complete in all the will of God" (Colossians 4:12). Every effort in the apostolic ministry moved toward the goal of presenting the people of God "in the unity of the faith, and of the knowledge of the Son of God, unto a perfect man, unto the measure of the stature of the fulness of Christ" (Ephesians 4:13).

No premium was given to spiritual dwarfs; no encouragement to an old babyhood. The babies were expected to grow; the old, instead of feebleness and infirmities, were to bear fruit in old age, and flourish. The divinest thing in religion is holy men and holy women.

No amount of money, genius, or culture can move the world for God. Holiness energizing the soul, the whole person aflame with love, with desire for more faith, more prayer, more zeal, more consecration—this is the secret of power. Christians must be the incarnation of this God-inflamed devotedness. God's advance has been stayed, his cause crippled, his name dishonored for their lack. Genius, education, position, dignity, place, honor, religious power cannot move this chariot of our God. It is a fiery one, and fiery forces only can move it.

The Devoted Life

Prayer is the creator as well as the channel of devotion. The spirit of devotion is the spirit of prayer. Prayer and devotion are united as soul and body are united, as life and heart are united. There is no real prayer without devotion, no devotion without real prayer. The Christian must be surrendered to God in the holiest devotion. Ministry is not a profession; it is a divine institution, a divine devotion. We must be devoted to God. Our aim, aspirations, ambitions must be for God and to God; prayer is as essential to devotion as food is to life.

The Christian, above everything else, must be devoted to God. Our relationship to God is the insignia and credential of our ministry. It must be clear, conclusive, unmistakable—no common, superficial piety. If we do not excel in grace, we do not excel at all. If we do not speak by life, character, conduct, we do not communicate truth at all. If our piety is shallow, our words may be as soft and as sweet as music, as gifted as Apollo, yet their impact will be fleeting, visionary, transient as the morning cloud or the early dew.

Character and Conduct

There is no substitute for devotion to God in the Christian's character and conduct. Devotion to a church, to opinions, to an organization, to orthodoxy are paltry, misleading, and vain when they become the source of inspiration. God must be the mainspring of the believer's effort, the fountain and crown of all toil. The name and honor of Jesus Christ, the advance of our cause, must be all in all. We must have no inspiration but the name of Jesus Christ, no ambition but to glorify him, no effort but for him. Then prayer will be a source of illumination, the means of perpetual advance, the gauge of our success. The only ambition the Christian can cherish is to have God with him.

Never did the cause of God need perfect illustrations of the possibilities of prayer more than in this age. No one will be an example of the gospel power except the person of deep and earnest prayer. A prayerless age will have scant models of divine power. Prayerless hearts will never rise to these heights. The age may be a better age than in the past, but there is an infinite distance between the improvement of an age by the force of advancing civilization and its improvement by the increase of holiness and Christlikeness through the energy of prayer.

The temple leaders in the time of Christ were much "better" in terms of external forms of righteousness than they were in ages before. They were in the golden age of their Pharisaic traditions. But their self-righteousness did not result in holiness—in fact, their Pharisaism crucified Christ.

Never was there more praying, but less prayer, than at that time. Never were there more sacrifices, but less sacrifice; never fewer idols, but greater idolatry; never more temple worship, but less God-worship. Never, in any age, was there more lip service, but less heart service to God—the lips gave honor to God while the hearts and hands crucified God's Son. Never were there more church-goers, but fewer saints than in that religious age.

Prayer-force makes saints. Holy characters and conduct are formed by the power of real praying. The more true saints, the more true prayer; the more prayer, the more saints.

Questions for Personal Insight and Group Discussion

Part 1: The Fullness of Christ

1. What does it mean to be "filled with all the fulness of God"?

2. How do I become "perfect and complete"? Is maturity a result of effort or a work of grace?

3. Bounds identifies the "divinest thing in religion" as "holy men and holy women." Why is the personal holiness of the believer so important to the spread of the gospel?

4. How does prayer accomplish what money, genius, and culture cannot?

Part 2: The Devoted Life

1. What is "devotion"? How is devotion to God demonstrated in my spiritual life?

2. How does "being devoted to God" differ from "having devotions"?

3 What does Bounds mean when he says, "There is no real prayer without devotion, no devotion without real prayer"?

4. How do I evaluate my level of devotion to God? How can I deepen my devotion to him?

Part 3: Character and Conduct

1. How does my devotion to God affect my character and my conduct? What other motives *besides* devotion to God motivate changes in my life?

2. Bounds says, "The only ambition the Christian can cherish is to have God with him." How does this single-minded

attitude relate to the other "ambitions" or goals in my life?

3.   Why was the religious fervor of the Pharisees not pleasing to God?   What kinds of Pharisaism exist in the church today?

4.   What is "lip service"? How does it differ from true devotion?

10

David Brainerd: An Example of Devotion

*I urge upon you communion with Christ, a growing commun-
ion . . . . Dig deep, and sweat and labor and take pains for him,
and set by as much time in the day for him as you can. He will
be won in the labor.*

—Samuel Rutherford

God has now, and has had many devoted, prayerful
people—men and women in whose lives prayer has
been a mighty, controlling, conspicuous force. The
world has felt their power. God has felt and honored
their power, and God's cause has moved mightily and
swiftly by their prayers. Holiness has shone out in their
characters with a divine radiance.

God found one such person in David Brainerd,
whose work and name have gone into history. He was
no ordinary man, but was capable of shining in any
company. Brainerd was the peer of the wise and gifted
ones, eminently suited to fill the most attractive pulpits
and to labor among the most refined and the cultured,
who were so anxious to secure him for their pastor.

Jonathan Edwards bore testimony of David Brainerd:

> [He was] a young man of distinguished talents, had extraordinary knowledge of men and things, had rare conversational powers, excelled in his knowledge of theology, and was truly, for one so young, an extraordinary divine, and especially in all matters relating to experimental religion. I never knew his equal of his stage and standing for clear and accurate notions of the nature and essence of true religion. His manner in prayer was almost inimitable, such as I have very rarely known equaled. His learning was very considerable, and he had extraordinary gifts for the pulpit.

No miracle attests the truth of Christianity with diviner force than the life and work of a man such as David Brainerd. Alone in the savage wilds of America, he struggled day and night with a mortal disease. He was unschooled in the care of souls, and often had access to the Indians only through the bungling medium of a pagan interpreter. But with the Word of God in his heart and in his hand, his soul fired with the divine flame, he poured out his soul to God in prayer. He fully established the worship of God and secured all its gracious results.

The Indians under his influence had their lives profoundly changed—they became pure, devout, intelligent Christians. Their vices reformed, they at once embraced and acted on the external duties of Christianity. Family prayer was established, the Sabbath instituted and faithfully observed; the internal graces of their faith were exhibited with growing sweetness and strength.

These results were not accidents of circumstance, but resulted from the outpouring of David Brainerd's life. He was God's man, for God first and last and all the time. God could flow freely through him. The omnipotence of grace was not hindered by the conditions of his heart; the whole channel was broadened and cleaned out for God's fullest and most powerful passage. Through Brainerd, God, with all his mighty forces, came down on the hopeless, savage wilderness and transformed it into a blooming and fruitful garden. Nothing is too hard for God to do if he can get the right kind of person to do it with.

Brainerd lived a life of holiness and prayer. His diary is full and monotonous with the record of his seasons of fasting, meditation, and retirement. He spent many hours in private prayer. "When I return home," he said, "and give myself to meditation, prayer, and fasting, my soul longs for mortification, self-denial, humility, and divorcement from all things of the world. I have nothing to do," he said, "with earth, but only to labor in it honestly for God. I do not desire to live one minute for anything which earth can afford."

After this high order Brainerd prayed:

> Feeling . . . the sweetness of communion with God and the constraining force of his love, and how admirably it captivates the soul and makes all the desires and affections to center in God, I set apart this day for secret fasting and prayer. . . . Near the middle of the afternoon God enabled me to wrestle ardently in intercession . . . but just at night the Lord visited me marvelously in prayer. . . . I felt no restraint, for the treasures of divine grace were opened to me.

Prayer gave David Brainerd's life and ministry their marvelous power.

The people of prayer are people of spiritual might. Prayers never die. Brainerd's whole life was a life of prayer; by day and by night he prayed—before and after preaching, riding through the interminable solitudes of the forest, on his bed of straw, in the dense and lonely forests, he prayed. Hour by hour, day after day, he was praying and fasting, pouring out his soul, interceding, communing with God.

Brainerd was with God mightily in prayer, and God was with him mightily. David Brainerd, being dead, still speaks and works, and will speak and work until the glorious day of our Lord.

Jonathan Edwards said of him:

> His life shows the right way to success in the works of the ministry. He sought it as the soldier seeks victory in a siege or battle; or as a man that runs a race for a great prize.... Like a true son of Jacob, he persevered in wrestling through all the darkness of the night, until the breaking of the day!

Questions for Personal Insight and Group Discussion

1. Why is David Brainerd an example of devotion to God? Are there other types of lifestyles that express equal devotion? Give examples.

2. What forms did Brainerd's devotion take?

3. What were the results of his commitment to God?

4. Is Brainerd's life merely the chronicle of an individual man's personal choices, or is it an example that modern Christians can follow?

5. Bounds says that Brainerd was "no ordinary man." In what ways is this statement true? In what ways is it not true? How does the "ordinariness" of Brainerd's life relate to his ministry?

6. What aspects of Brainerd's life experience are his alone? What aspects can I apply to my own walk with God?

11

Heart
Preparation

Nothing reaches the heart but what is from the heart, or pierces the conscience but what comes from a living conscience.

—William Penn

The Heart of Prayer

How manifold, illimitable, valuable, and helpful prayer is to the minister! Prayer puts heart into the minister's words, and puts the minister's words into the heart. Men and women of great hearts have great influence for the kingdom of God. People of bad hearts may do a measure of good, but this is rare. The hireling and the stranger may help the sheep at some points, but it is the good shepherd with the good shepherd's heart who will bless the sheep and fulfill the shepherd's place.*

---

* In John 10:1-18, Jesus describes the "Good Shepherd" who gives himself for his flock, the hireling who cares only for his pay, the thief who climbs in over the wall, and the wolf who seeks to devour the sheep. Bounds draws a number of images from this passage.

We have lost sight of the importance of preparing our hearts. A prepared heart is better than a prepared teaching, for a prepared heart will result in a prepared teaching.

Volumes have been written laying down the mechanics of ministry-building, until we have become possessed with the idea that the scaffolding is the building. The young minister has been taught to lay out all his strength on the form, taste, and beauty of his ministry as a mechanical and intellectual product. We have thereby cultivated a vicious taste among the people and raised the clamor for talent instead of grace, eloquence instead of piety, rhetoric instead of revelation, reputation and brilliance instead of holiness. And we have lost the true idea of ministry, lost preaching power, lost conviction for sin, lost the rich experience and elevated Christian character, lost the authority over consciences and lives which always results from genuine ministry.

Heart Failure

We must not assume that our leaders study too much. Some of them do not study at all; others do not study enough. Many do not study in the right way to show themselves approved of God (2 Timothy 2:15). But our great lack is not in head culture, but in heart culture; not lack of knowledge but lack of holiness is our sad and telling defect—not that we know too much, but that we do not meditate on God and his Word and watch and fast and pray enough.

The heart is the great hindrance in our ministry. Words pregnant with divine truth find no passage in our hearts; arrested, they die powerless.

Can ambition, that lusts after praise and position,

speak the gospel of him who made himself of no reputation and took on him the form of a servant? (Philippians 2:7). Can the proud, the vain, the egotistical minister the gospel of him who was meek and lowly? Can the
bad-tempered, passionate, selfish, hard, worldly person offer the life which teems with long-suffering, self-
denial, tenderness, which imperatively demands separation from enmity and crucifixion to the world? Can
the hireling official—heartless and perfunctory—communicate the gospel which demands the shepherd to
give his life for the sheep? (John 10:11-13). Can the
covetous one, who counts salary and money, minister
the gospel in the spirit of Christ and Paul and the words
of Wesley: "I count it dung and dross; I trample it under
my feet; I (yet not I, but the grace of God in me) esteem
it just as the mire of the streets, and I desire it not, I seek
it not"?**

A Child's Heart

God's revelation does not need the light of human
genius, the polish and strength of human culture, the
brilliance of human thought, the force of human brains
to adorn or enforce it. But it does demand the simplicity,
the docility, humility, and faith of a child's heart.

This surrender and subordination of intellect and
genius to the divine and spiritual forces made Paul

** Wesley's quotation echoes the words of Paul in Philippians
3:7-8: "But what things were gain to me, those I counted loss for
Christ. Yea doubtless, and I count all things but loss for the
excellency of the knowledge of Christ Jesus my Lord: for whom I
have suffered the loss of all things, and do count them but dung,
that I may win Christ."

unequaled among the apostles. This same surrender gave Wesley his power and established his labors in the history of humanity. Such childlike trust gave Loyola the strength to arrest the retreating forces of Catholicism.

Our great need is heart preparation. Luther held it as an axiom: "He who has prayed well has studied well." We need not abandon our intellects, of course; but we use our minds best when we cultivate our hearts most. We should be students, but our great study should be the Bible, and we study the Bible best when we keep our hearts with diligence. We should not avoid knowing humanity, but we will be more adept in human nature when we have fathomed the depths and intricacies of our own heart.

While the channel of ministry is the mind, its fountain is the heart. We may broaden and deepen the channel, but if we do not see to the purity and depth of the fountain, we will have dry or polluted channels.

Almost anyone of common intelligence has sense enough to communicate the gospel, but very few have grace enough to do so. Those who have struggled with their own hearts and conquered, who have humility, faith, love, truth, mercy, sympathy, courage; who can pour the rich treasures of the heart through the intellect, charged with the power of the gospel—such people will be the truest, most successful ministers of the gospel in the esteem of their Lord.

Questions for Personal Insight and Group Discussion

Part 1: The Heart of Prayer

1.   Why is the preparation of the heart so important in ministering the gospel?

2.   Is Bounds recommending that we abandon study and preparation in favor of prayer? Why or why not?

3.   In what ways do we "mistake the scaffolding for the building" where ministry is concerned? Give examples.

4.   What do most people look for in a "successful" pastor or preacher? What does God look for?

Part 2: Heart Failure

1.   Bounds says our lack is "not lack of knowledge but lack of holiness." What is the difference between knowledge and holiness?

2.   What kinds of "hirelings" are evident in the church today? How do I know they are hirelings? What kind of ministries do such people have?

3.   How do pride, selfishness, and greed hinder the communication of the true gospel?

Part 3: A Child's Heart

1.   What does it mean to have the "faith of a child's heart"? What is the difference between childlikeness and childishness?

2.   Is Bounds anti-intellectual in his approach to ministry? Why or why not?

3. Why is prayer more important than preparation to a fruitful ministry?

4. Bounds says, "Almost anyone of common intelligence has sense enough to communicate the gospel, but very few have grace enough to do so." What does this mean? How does it apply to my own life and ministry?

12

Heart and Head

Study not to be a fine preacher. Jerichos are blown down with rams' horns. Look simply unto Jesus for preaching food; and what is wanted will be given. . . . Your mouth will be a flowing stream or a fountain sealed, according as your heart is.

—John Berridge

Heart Forces

The heart is the savior of the world. Heads do not save. Genius, brains, brilliance, strength, natural gifts do not save. The gospel flows through hearts. All the most powerful forces are heart forces. All the sweetest and loveliest graces are heart graces. Great hearts make great characters; great hearts make divine characters.

God is love. There is nothing greater than love, nothing greater than God. Hearts make heaven; heaven is love. There is nothing higher, nothing sweeter, than heaven. And thus it is the heart and not the head which determines the great men and women of God. The heart counts for everything. The heart must speak from the pulpit; it must hear from the pew. We serve God with our hearts—head homage does not serve in heaven.

One of the serious errors of the modern pulpit is the intrusion of more thought than prayer, of more head than heart. The pastor binds his people to him and governs his people by his heart. They may admire his gifts, they may be proud of his ability, they may be affected for a time by his sermons; but the stronghold of his power is his heart. His scepter is love. The throne of his power is his heart.

The good shepherd gives his life for the sheep. Heads never make martyrs; it is the heart which surrenders the life to love and fidelity. It takes great courage to be a faithful pastor, but the heart alone can supply this courage. Gifts and genius may abound, but only the gifts and genius of the heart and not the head count for God's kingdom.

"Give Me Thine Heart"

It is easier to fill the head than to prepare the heart. But heart drew the Son of God from heaven, and heart will draw people to heaven. The world desperately needs men and women of heart to sympathize with its woe, to kiss away its sorrows, to show compassion in its misery, to alleviate its pain. Christ was eminently the man of sorrows because he was pre-eminently the man of heart.

"Give me thine heart," is God's requisition of men (Proverbs 23:26). "Give me thine heart" is also humanity's demand of us.

A professional ministry is a heartless ministry. When salary plays a great part in the ministry, the heart plays little part. We may make ministry our business, and not put our hearts into the business. If we put self to the front, we put heart to the rear. If we do not sow with our hearts, we will never reap a harvest for God. "Jesus wept" (John 11:35) is the shortest and biggest verse in the Bible. Those who go forth *weeping* (not preaching great sermons), bearing precious seed, shall come again rejoicing, bringing their sheaves with them (Psalm 126:6).

Praying gives sense, brings wisdom, broadens and strengthens the mind. The closet of prayer is the perfect school-teacher and school-house for the servant of Christ. Thought is not only brightened and clarified in prayer, but thought is born in prayer. We can learn more in an hour praying, when praying indeed, than from many hours studying. Books are in the closet which can be found and read nowhere else. Revelations are made in the closet which are made nowhere else.

Questions for Personal Insight and Group Discussion

Part 1: Heart Forces

1. Why does Bounds say that the "heart is the savior of the world"? In what ways is this true?

2. How does a pastor govern people by the heart? What difference does the heart of a pastor make to the congregation?

3. What kind of surrender is necessary if we wish to serve Christ from the heart?

4. What is the condition of my own heart? How does that affect my ministry to others?

Part 2: "Give Me Thine Heart"

1.   How does the world respond to people of great genius? To people of great heart?

2.   Are there modern examples of people who are personally affecting the world mightily because of their great hearts? Give examples. Why are these people so influential?

3.   How does Psalm 126:5-6 relate to heart ministry?

4.   How can we learn more in one hour of praying than we can from many hours of study? Have I ever experienced that truth in my own prayer life?

13

Anointing

If the anointing which we bear come not from the Lord of hosts,
we are deceivers, since only in prayer can we obtain it. Let us
continue instant, constant, fervent in supplication.

—Charles Haddon Spurgeon

The Anointed Word

Alexander Knox, a Christian philosopher of the days of
Wesley, not an adherent but a strong personal friend of
Wesley, wrote:

> It is strange and lamentable, but I verily believe the fact to be
> that except among Methodist and Methodistical clergymen,
> there is not much interesting preaching in England. There
> is, I conceive, in the great laws of the moral world a kind of
> secret understanding like the affinities in chemistry, be-
> tween rightly promulgated religious truth and the deepest
> feelings of the human mind. Where the one is duly exhib-
> ited, the other will respond. . . .
>   I felt real pleasure last Sunday. I can bear witness that

the preacher did at once speak the words of truth and soberness. There was no eloquence—the honest man never dreamed of such a thing—but there was far better: a cordial communication of vitalized truth. I say vitalized because what he declared to others it was impossible not to feel he lived on himself.

The anointing, or unction, to which Knox refers is the art of preaching, the empowering behind ministry. Whatever other arts we may have and retain—the art of sermon-making, the art of eloquence, the art of great, clear thinking, the art of pleasing an audience—these are nothing without the anointing of the Holy Spirit. Anointing makes God's truth powerful and interesting, draws and attracts, edifies, convicts, and saves.

The Spiritual Difference

The anointing revitalizes God's truth, makes it living and life-giving. Even God's truth spoken without the anointing of the Spirit is light, dead, and deadening. It may abound in truth, weighty with thought, sparkling with rhetoric, pointed in logic, powerful in earnestness, but without this divine anointing, it issues in death and not in life.

Spurgeon said:

I wonder how long we might beat our brains before we could plainly put into word what is meant by preaching with unction. Yet he who preaches knows its presence, and he who hears soon detects its absence. . . . Everyone knows what the freshness of the morning is when orient pearls abound on every blade of grass, but who can describe it, much less produce it of itself? Such is the mystery of spiritual anointing. We know, but we cannot tell to others what it is. Unction is a thing which you cannot manufacture. . . . It is, in itself, priceless and beyond measure needful if you would edify believers and bring sinners to Christ.

Anointing is that indefinable, indescribable something which makes the word of God "quick, and powerful, and sharper than any two-edged sword, piercing even to the dividing asunder of soul and spirit, and of the joints and marrow, and . . . a discerner of the thoughts and intents of the heart" (Hebrews 4:12). Anointing gives the words of the speaker point, sharpness, and power; it creates friction and stir in many a dead congregation.

The same truths may have been told in the strictness of the letter, smooth as human oil could make them; but no signs of life, not a pulse throb; all as peaceful as the grave and as dead. When the minister meanwhile receives an anointing, the letter of the Word is embellished and fired by this mysterious power, and the throbbings of life begin—life which receives or life which resists. The anointing pervades and convicts the conscience and breaks the heart.

The divine anointing is the feature which separates and distinguishes true gospel preaching from all other methods of presenting the truth, and which creates a wide spiritual chasm between the one who has it and the one who does not. It fires revealed truth with all the energy of God. Anointing is simply the Spirit of God infusing his own Word and his own servant. It inspires and clarifies the intellect, gives insight and grasp and projecting power; it gives to the believer heart power, which is greater than head power; and tenderness, purity, force flow from the heart by it. Enlargement, freedom, fullness of thought, directness, and simplicity of utterance are the fruits of this anointing.

Earnestness vs. Anointing

Often earnestness is mistaken for anointing. The one who has divine anointing will be earnest in the very spiritual nature of things, but there may be great earnestness without the least bit of anointing.

Earnestness and anointing look alike from some points of view. Earnestness may be readily and without detection substituted or mistaken for anointing. It requires a spiritual eye and a spiritual taste to discriminate.

Earnestness may be sincere, serious, ardent, and persevering. It goes at a task with good will, pursues it with perseverance, and urges it with ardor. But all these forces do not rise higher than the merely human. Human effort is in it—the whole person, with will and heart, brain and genius, planning and working and talking.

There may be little of God in it. There may, in fact, be none of God in it because there is so much of the human in it. We please or touch and move or overwhelm with conviction, and in all this earnestness we may move along earthly ways, being propelled by human forces only. The altar is made by earthly hands and its fire kindled by earthly flames. We grow exceedingly earnest over our own plans or movements, but earnestness may be only selfishness.

Anointing, however, distinguishes and separates true ministry from all mere human efforts. It is the divine in ministry. It makes the Word sharp to those who need sharpening. It distills as the dew to those who need to be refreshed.

Anointing comes not to the study but to the closet. It is heaven's answer to prayer, the sweetest exhalation of the Holy Spirit. It suffuses, softens, cuts, and soothes. It carries the Word like dynamite, like salt, like sugar; it makes the Word a healer, an arraigner, a revealer, a searcher; it makes the hearer a culprit or a saint, makes him weep like a child and live like a giant.

The anointing is not the gift of genius. It is not found in the halls of learning. No eloquence can woo it. No industry can win it. No hands can confer it. It is the gift of God—the royal signet given to the King's own messengers. It is heaven's knighthood offered to the chosen true and brave ones who have sought this honor through many an hour of tearful, wrestling prayer.

Earnestness is good and impressive; genius is gifted and great. Thought kindles and inspires, but it takes a diviner endowment, a more powerful energy than earnestness or genius or thought to break the chains of sin, to win estranged and depraved hearts to God, to repair the breaches and restore the church to her old ways of purity and power. Nothing but the anointing of the Holy Spirit can do this.

Questions for Personal Insight and Group Discussion

Part 1: The Anointed Word

1. What does "anointing" mean in regard to ministry? How can I tell if a speaker's words or plans are anointed?

2. What is the difference between anointing and emotionalism? Why is anointing not a function of human ability?

3. What does anointing accomplish in a worship service? Why is it necessary to real worship?

4. What is the role of anointing in conviction of sin and salvation?

Part 2: The Spiritual Difference

1. Have I ever experienced true anointing in corporate worship? In my private prayer life? When, and under what circumstances?

2. What happens to the Word of God when the speaker is anointed by the Spirit? Why?

3. Is hearing an anointed message always a comfortable experience? Why or why not?

4. What are the results of anointed ministry?

Part 3: Earnestness vs. Anointing

1. What is the difference between earnestness and anointing? How can a speaker, or the listener, discern the differences?

2. Can a word be anointed for the speaker and not for the listener? Can it be anointed for the hearer when the speaker is merely earnest? Why or why not?

3. Where does anointing come from? How does a person get it?

4. Is anointing important only for public ministry, or is it also applicable for my daily life? What does anointing mean in my daily experience of knowing and serving God?

14

Prayer and the Spirit's Power

Unction must come down from heaven and spread a savor and feeling and relish over . . . ministry; . . . the Bible must hold the first place, and the last also must be given to the Word of God and prayer.

—Richard Cecil

Set Apart for God

In Christian terms, "unction" is the anointing of the Holy Ghost, separating unto God's work and qualifying for it. This anointing is the one divine enablement by which the Christian accomplishes God's purposes. Without this anointing no true spiritual results are accomplished; the results and forces in ministry do not rise above the results of unsanctified speech and action.

Through the Word of God, this divine anointing generates spiritual results that flow from the gospel; without this anointing, no such results are secured. Many pleasant impressions may be made, but these all fall far below the ends of gospel ministry. The fervor or softness excited by an emotional sermon may look like the movements of the divine anointing, but they have no penetrating, heart-breaking force. No heart-healing balm arises from these surface, sympathetic, emotional movements. They are not radical in any way—neither sin-searching nor sin-curing.

Divine anointing is the one distinguishing feature that separates true gospel preaching from all other methods of presenting truth. The Spirit backs and interpenetrates the revealed truth with all the force of God. Anointing illuminates the Word and broadens and enriches the intellect, empowering it to grasp and apprehend the Word. It qualifies the spiritual leader's heart, and brings it to that condition of tenderness, purity, force, and light necessary to result in godly changes. This anointing gives us liberty and enlargement of thought and soul—a freedom, fullness, and directness of speech that can be secured by no other process.

Without this anointing the gospel has no more power to propagate itself than any other system of truth. This is the seal of its divinity. Anointing in the speaker puts God in the gospel. Without anointing God is absent, and the gospel is left to the low and unsatisfactory forces that human ingenuity, interest, or talents can devise to enforce and project its doctrines.

Ministry more often fails in anointing than in any other element. Learning may enlighten, brilliance and eloquence may delight and charm, sensation may bring the populace in crowds, mental powers may impress; but without the anointing of the Holy Spirit, all these will be like the fretful assault of the waters on Gibraltar. Spray and foam may cover and spangle, but the rocks remain, unimpressed and unimpressible. The human heart can no more be swept of its hardness and sin by human forces than these rocks can be swept away by the ocean's ceaseless flow.

Heavenly anointing is the consecration force, and its presence is a continual test of that consecration. This anointing secures the Christian's consecration to God and to his work. Other forces and motives may call a person, but a separation to God's work by the power of the Holy Spirit is the only consecration recognized by God as legitimate.

Anointing is essential to real spiritual change. The divine and heavenly oil put on it by the imposition of God's hand must soften the whole person—head, heart, spirit—until it separates the believer from all earthly, secular, worldly, selfish motives and aims, setting the Christian apart to everything that is pure and Godlike.

Daily Manna

The anointing and empowering of the Holy Spirit is not a memory of an era of the past; it is a present, realized, conscious fact. It belongs to the experience of every man and woman, as well as to each Christian's ministry. Anointing transforms the believer into the image of the divine Master, and gives power to the truths of Christ. It is so much the power in the ministry as to make all else seem feeble and vain without it, and by its presence to atone for the absence of all other forces.

This anointing is not an inalienable right. It is a conditional gift, and its presence is perpetuated and increased by the same process by which it was at first secured—by unceasing prayer to God, by impassioned desire after God, by honoring it, by seeking it with tireless ardor, by deeming all else loss and failure without it.

Prayer, much prayer, is the price of anointing. Prayer, much prayer, is the sole condition of keeping it. Without this unceasing prayer the anointing never comes. Without perseverance in prayer, the anointing, like manna overkept, breeds worms (Exodus 16:4-20).

Praying hearts are the only hearts filled with this holy oil; only praying lips are anointed with this divine power.

Questions for Personal Insight and Group Discussion

Part 1: Set Apart for God

1. What does it mean to be "sanctified" or "set apart" for God's purposes?

2. When we are "set apart" by the Spirit, from what are we separated? Does separation mean holding ourselves apart from unbelievers? Why or why not?

3. How does the anointing of the Holy Spirit separate "true gospel preaching from all other methods of presenting truth"? What does it mean for the intellect to be "empowered"?

4. How does the anointing of the Holy Spirit separate me from sin? How does it set me apart for the purposes of God?

Part 2: Daily Manna

1. Why is the anointing of the Holy Spirit on ministry just as important today as it was in the past?

2. What does Bounds mean when he says, "This anointing is not an inalienable right. It is a conditional gift"?

3. Why is prayer the essential factor in appropriating the anointing of the Holy Spirit for daily life and ministry?

4. How is the story of manna in the wilderness (Exodus 16) an analogy of the work of the Holy Spirit?

15

Spiritual Leadership

Give me one hundred preachers who fear nothing but sin and desire nothing but God, and I care not a straw whether they be clergymen or laymen; such alone will shake the gates of hell and set up the kingdom of heaven on earth. God does nothing but in answer to prayer.

—John Wesley

Priorities in Prayer

The apostles knew the necessity and worth of prayer to their ministry. They knew that their high commission as apostles, instead of relieving them from the necessity of prayer, committed them to it by a more urgent need. They were exceedingly careful lest some other important work should exhaust their time and prevent them from praying as they ought. Thus they appointed laymen to look after the delicate and engrossing duties of ministering to the poor, so that the apostles might, unhindered, give themselves "continually to prayer, and to the ministry of the word" (Acts 6:1-4).

Prayer is put first, and they give themselves to it, making a priority of it, surrendering themselves to prayer, putting fervor, urgency, perseverance, and time in it.

The apostles devoted themselves to this divine work of prayer. "Night and day praying exceedingly," (1 Thessalonians 3:10) Paul describes his habit of prayer. "We will give ourselves continually to prayer," (Acts 6:4) the apostles concluded. These New Testament leaders wholeheartedly committed themselves to prayer for God's people. They put God in full force into their churches by their praying.

These holy apostles did not vainly fancy that they had met their high and solemn duties by delivering God's word faithfully, but their preaching was made effective and fruitful by the ardor and insistence of their praying.

Apostolic praying was as taxing, toilsome, and imperative as apostolic preaching. They prayed mightily day and night to bring their people to the highest regions of faith and holiness. They prayed mightier still to hold them to this high spiritual altitude.

Christians who have never learned in the school of Christ the high and divine art of intercession for those under their leadership will never truly learn the art of ministry.

Praying Leaders

The prayers of saintly leaders do much in making saints of those who follow them. If the church leaders in later years had been as particular and fervent in praying for their people as the apostles were, the dark times of worldliness and apostasy might not have marred the history, eclipsed the glory, and arrested the advancement of the church. Apostolic praying makes apostolic saints and keeps apostolic purity and power in the church.

Loftiness of soul, purity and elevation of motive, unselfishness, self-sacrifice, exhaustive toil, ardor of spirit, and divine tact are required to be an intercessor for others. The Christian is to dedicate time and effort in prayer for the people; not simply that they might be saved, but that they might be mightily saved.

The apostles gave themselves to prayer that their saints might be perfect; not that they should have a little enthusiasm for the things of God, but that they "might be filled with all the fulness of God" (Ephesians 3:19). Paul did not rely on his preaching to secure the salvation of those in his charge, but "for this cause" he bowed his "knees unto the Father of our Lord Jesus Christ" (Ephesians 3:14). Paul's prayer carried Paul's converts farther along the highway of sainthood than his preaching ever did.

Epaphras did as much or more by prayer for the Colossian saints than by his preaching. He labored fervently always in prayer for them that they might "stand perfect and complete in all the will of God" (Colossians 4:12).

Pastors and preachers are pre-eminent among God's leaders. They are primarily responsible for the condition of the church. They shape its character, give tone and direction to its life.

Much depends upon these leaders. They influence the times and the institutions. The church is divine, the treasure it holds is heavenly, but it bears the imprint of the human. The treasure is in earthen vessels, and it is marked by the vessel. The church of God makes, or is made by, its leaders. Whether it makes them or is made by them, it will be what its leaders are—spiritual if they are holy, secular if they are worldly.

Israel's kings determined Israel's piety. A church rarely revolts against or rises above the religion of its leaders. Strongly spiritual leaders, men and women of holy might, at the lead, are tokens of God's favor. Disaster and weakness follow in the wake of feeble or worldly leadership. As Israel's history demonstrates, times of spiritual leadership are times of great spiritual prosperity for the church.

Prayer is one of the primary characteristics of strong spiritual leadership. People of powerful prayer are people who mold history. Their power with God has the conquering tread.

How can a Christian minister who does not get the Word fresh from God in daily prayer? How can we speak without having our faith quickened, our vision cleared, and our hearts warmed in communion with God? Lips which are untouched by the flame of God's presence will ever be dry and motionless. Divine truth will never issue with power from such lips.

A prayerless ministry is the undertaker for God's truth and for God's church. We may have the most costly casket and the most beautiful flowers, but it is a funeral nevertheless. Ages of millennial glory have been lost by prayerlessness; the coming of our Lord has been postponed indefinitely by lack of prayer, and hell has enlarged and filled its dire caves in the presence of the dead service of a prayerless church.

The best, the greatest offering we can give is the offering of prayer. If leaders of the twentieth century will learn well the lesson of prayer, and use fully the power of prayer, the millennium will come before the century closes.

"Pray without ceasing" (1 Thessalonians 5:17) is the trumpet call to leaders of the twentieth century. If the twentieth century will get their words, their thoughts, their ministry from the prayer closet, the next century will find a new heaven and a new earth. The old sin-stained and sin-eclipsed heaven and earth will pass away under the power of a praying ministry.

Questions for Personal Insight and Group Discussion

Part 1: Priorities in Prayer

1. What does "giving myself continually to prayer" mean? How, in practical terms, can I do this amid the activities of my life?

2. What is the importance of prayer to the Christian leader?

3. What is a leader? Who are my spiritual leaders? In what circumstances, or in whose lives, am I a leader?

4. As a leader, what responsibilities do I have to those under my care? As a follower, what responsibilities do I have to my leaders?

Part 2: Praying Leaders

1. According to Ephesians 4:11-12, what is the purpose of leadership? Who is to do the work of the ministry? Where do I fit into that plan?

2. Is there a different standard of holiness for Christian leaders than for "ordinary" Christians? In what way?

3. How does a Christian leader shape the church? How does the church shape the leader?

4. How does the prayer of the Christian in the pew affect the ministry of the Christian in the pulpit?

16

Praying
for Leaders

If some Christians that have been complaining of their ministers had. . . risen and stormed heaven with their humble, fervent, and incessant prayers for them, they would have been much more in the way of success.

—Jonathan Edwards

Prayer for the Pastor

Prayer, to the pastor or preacher, is not simply the duty of his profession, a privilege; it is a necessity, like air to the lungs. It is absolutely necessary for the spiritual leader to pray. And it is equally necessary that the leader be prayed for. These two propositions are wedded into a union which ought never to know any divorce: *the leader must pray; the leader must be prayed for.*

Prayer is essential to meet all the fearful responsibilities and gain the largest, truest success in the work of ministry. The true leader, next to the cultivation of the spirit and practice of personal prayer, needs the prayers of God's people.

The holier our leaders are, the more they estimate prayer; they see that God gives himself to those who pray, and that his revelation of himself is in proportion to the soul's longing prayer to God. Salvation never comes to a prayerless heart. The Holy Spirit never abides in a prayerless spirit. Preaching never edifies a prayerless soul. Christ knows nothing of prayerless Christians.

Likewise, the gospel cannot be projected by a prayerless leader. Gifts, talents, education, eloquence, even God's call, cannot abate the need for prayer. These factors only intensify the necessity for the leader to pray and to be prayed for. The more our leaders' eyes are open to the nature, responsibility, and difficulty of the work of ministry, the more they recognize the necessity of prayer; not only the demand for personal prayer, but the need to call on others to help with their prayers.

The Call for Prayer

If any man could project the gospel by virtue of personal force, brain power, culture, personal grace, apostolic commission, or God's extraordinary call, that man was Paul. Yet Paul is an eminent example that the true leader must give himself to prayer and have the prayers of others as well. He asks, he covets, he pleads in an impassioned way for the help of all God's saints.

Paul knew that in the spiritual realm, as elsewhere, in union there is strength. In the concentration of faith, desire, and prayer came the increase of spiritual force until it became overwhelming and irresistible in its power. Units of prayer combine, like drops of water, to make an ocean which defies resistance. So Paul, with his clear and full apprehension of spiritual dynamics, determined to make his ministry as impressive, as eternal, as irresistible as the ocean. Paul's pre-eminence in labor and results, in influence on the church and the world, is found in the fact that he was able to center himself and his ministry on the prayers of others.

To his brethren at Rome he wrote: "Now I beseech you, brethren, for the Lord Jesus Christ's sake, and for the love of the Spirit, that ye strive together with me in your prayers to God for me" (Romans 15:30). To the Ephesians he said: "Praying always with all prayer and supplication in the Spirit, and watching thereunto with all perseverance and supplication for all saints; And for me, that utterance may be given unto me, that I may open my mouth boldly, to make known the mystery of the gospel" (Ephesians 6:18-19). To the Colossians he emphasized: "Withal praying also for us, that God would open unto us a door of utterance, to speak the mystery of Christ, for which I am also in bonds: That I may make it manifest, as I ought to speak" (Colossians 4:3).

To the Thessalonians he said sharply, strongly: "Brethren, pray for us" (1 Thessalonians 5:25). Paul also called on the Corinthian church to help him: "Ye also helping together by prayer for us" (2 Corinthians 1:11). This was to be part of their work; they were to contribute the helping hand of prayer. In an additional and closing charge to the Thessalonian church about the importance and necessity of their prayers, Paul said: "Finally, brethren, pray for us, that the word of the Lord may have free course, and be glorified, even as it is with you: And that we may be delivered from unreasonable and wicked men" (2 Thessalonians 3:1-2).

Paul further impressed upon the Philippians that all his trials and opposition can be made subservient to the spread of the gospel by their prayers for him (Philippians 1:19). And to Philemon, he commanded that a lodging be prepared for him, trusting that through Philemon's prayer Paul would be his guest (Philemon 22).

The Effect of Prayer

Paul's attitude on this question illustrates his humility and his deep insight into the spiritual forces which project the gospel. And it teaches a lesson for all times: if Paul was so dependent upon the prayers of God's saints to give his ministry success, how much greater the necessity that the prayers of God's people be centered on the ministry today!

Paul did not feel that this urgent plea for prayer lowered his dignity, lessened his influence, or depreciated his piety. But what if it did? Let dignity go, let influence be destroyed, let his reputation be marred—he must have their prayers. Called, commissioned, chief of the apostles, all Paul's equipment was imperfect without the prayers of his people. He wrote letters everywhere, urging people to pray for him.

Do we pray for our leaders? Do we pray for them in secret? Public prayers are of little worth unless they are founded on and followed up by private praying. The praying ones are to the leader as Aaron and Hur were to Moses—they hold up the hands that decide the outcome of the battle raging around them (Exodus 17:11-13).

The plea and purpose of the apostles put the church to praying. They did not ignore the grace of cheerful giving; they were not ignorant of the place of religious activity and work in the spiritual life. But none of these could compare in necessity and importance with prayer.

The most sacred and urgent pleas, the most fervent exhortations, the most arousing words were uttered to enforce the all-important obligation and necessity of prayer.

Questions for Personal Insight and Group Discussion

Part 1: Prayer for the Pastor

1. Is praying for our spiritual leaders an admission of their insufficiency? What is the importance of praying for them?

2. When trouble arises in the fellowship, am I more likely to complain, or to pray? Why?

3. Bounds says, "The holier our leaders are, the more they estimate prayer." What does he mean? Why does prayer become more important as we draw closer to the Lord?

4. Who are the people who have spiritual leadership in my life? What are their needs? How can I pray for them?

Part 2: The Call for Prayer

1. Why did Paul, the greatest of leaders in the church, ask for prayers from others?

2. What does Paul's desire for prayer support teach me about the importance of praying for my leaders?

3. How is prayer a "partnership" in the ministry?

4. What effect does prayer for my leaders have on their ministry? On my attitudes?

Part 3: The Effect of Prayer

1.   Often we express frustration over our inability to change circumstances by saying, "There's nothing I can do but pray." Why do we often consider prayer as a "last resort" to more tangible action? Does the Scripture support this attitude?

2.   Is prayer a substitute for action? What is the relationship between prayer and action?

3.   Consider the ministry of Aaron and Hur in Exodus 17:11-13. In what way do I "hold up the hands" of God's prophets and leaders?

4.   What changes can I make in my attitudes and practice to be more supportive of the spiritual leaders God has put into my life?

17

Deliberate Prayer

*This perpetual hurry of business and company ruins me in soul
if not in body. . . . Without a due measure of private devotions
the soul will grow lean.*

—William Wilberforce

Waiting Upon the Lord

Our devotions are not measured by the clock, but time
is of their essence. The ability to wait and stay and press
belongs essentially to our communication with God.
Hurry, to an alarming extent, damages our communion
with the Lord. Short devotions are the bane of deep
piety. Calmness, grasp, strength, are never the compan-
ions of hurry. Short devotions deplete spiritual vigor,
arrest spiritual progress, sap spiritual foundations, blight
the root and bloom of spiritual life. They are the prolific
source of backsliding, the sure indication of superficial
piety. They deceive, blight, rot the seed, and impoverish
the soil.

Bible prayers in word and print are short, but the praying men of the Bible were with God through many a sweet and holy wrestling hour. They won by few words but long waiting. The prayers Moses records may be short, but Moses prayed to God with fasting forty days and nights (Exodus 24:18; Deuteronomy 9:9).

The statement of Elijah's praying may be condensed to a few brief paragraphs, but doubtless Elijah spent many hours of fiery struggle and lofty interchange with God before he could, with assured boldness, say to Ahab, "There shall not be dew nor rain these years, but according to my word" (1 Kings 17:1).

The verbal brief of Paul's prayers is short, but Paul was "night and day praying exceedingly" (1 Thessalonians 3:10). The Lord's Prayer is a divine example for infant lips, but the man Christ Jesus prayed many nights before his work was done; and his all-night devotions gave to his work its finish and perfection, and to his character the fullness and glory of its divinity (Luke 6:12).

Spiritual work is taxing work. Praying, true praying, costs an outlay of serious attention and of time, which flesh and blood do not relish. Few persons are made of such strong fiber that they willingly give their all when a surface effort will do. We can accustom ourselves to mediocre praying until it looks acceptable to us. At least it keeps up a decent form and quiets the conscience. But such a habit is a deadly opiate; we can neglect prayer and not notice the danger until the foundations are gone.

Hurried devotions make weak faith, feeble convictions, questionable piety. To cut short our praying makes the whole religious character puny and powerless.

It takes time for the full flow of God into the spirit. Short devotions cut the pipe of God's full flow. It takes time in the secret places to get the full revelation of God. Hurry and distraction mar the picture.

Henry Martyn lamented that "want of private devotional reading and shortness of prayer through incessant sermon-making had produced much strangeness between God and his soul." He judged that he had dedicated too much time to *public* ministry and too little to *private* communion with God.

Total Devotion

More time and early hours for prayer might work miracles to revive and invigorate many a decayed spiritual life, manifesting in holy living. A holy life would not be so rare or difficult if our devotions were not so short and hurried. A Christlike character would not be so alien and hopeless a heritage if our prayers were lengthened and intensified. We live shabbily because we pray poorly. Our ability to stay with God in the closet measures our ability to stay with him out of the closet.

We are not only deluded by brevity in devotions; we are losers in many ways and in many rich legacies. We are taught in prayer, and the greatest victories are often the results of great waiting—waiting until words and plans are exhausted, and silent patience gains the crown.

To pray is the greatest thing we can do; and to do it well we must have calmness, time, and deliberation. True praying has the largest results for good, and poor praying, the least. We cannot do too much real praying; we cannot do too little of the shame.

We must learn anew the worth of prayer, enter anew the school of prayer. There is nothing which takes more time to learn. And if we would learn the wondrous art, we must not give a fragment here and there—"A little talk with Jesus," as the tiny saintlets sing. We must demand and hold with iron grasp the best hours of the day for God and for prayer, or there will be no praying worth the name.

This generation, however, is not an age of prayer. Few pray; prayer is defamed by preacher and priest. In these days of hurry and bustle, people do not take the time to pray. Preachers "say prayers" as part of their program, but who stirs himself up to take hold upon God? (Isaiah 64:7)

Many will give of their money—some in rich abundance—but they will not "give themselves" as the apostles did to prayer, without which their money is only a curse. Many will deliver great and eloquent addresses on the need for revival and the spread of the kingdom of God, but few will pray—and without prayer all preaching and organizing are worse than vain. Prayer is a lost art; the greatest benefactor this age could have is the one who will call the leaders and the church back to prayer.

Questions for Personal Insight and Group Discussion

Part 1: Waiting Upon the Lord

1. How does "hurry" interfere with my personal prayer life? What can I do about it?

2. Why is extended time necessary for an outpouring of God's presence and power?

3. Have I ever experienced a real release in prayer, so that time seemed to stand still and the Lord's presence was overwhelming? What effect does such an experience have on my desire to pray?

4. Are the prayer lives of people like Elijah, Moses, Paul, and David Brainerd realistic choices for imitation? Who do I know personally whose prayer life inspires me? How can I take practical steps to improve my own devotional time with God?

Part 2: Total Devotion

1. What does the "image of Christ" look like? How can I become more Christlike in my own life?

2. What does it mean to "wait on the Lord"? How can I rid my mind of the thousand distractions that hinder my concentration on God?

3. Are most church prayer meetings "real prayer" as Bounds defines it? What can I do to bring more depth and reality to prayer times in my fellowship?

4. What does it mean for God to speak to me? What do I expect to happen when I spend time in prayer with the Lord?

18

Praying Pulpit, Praying Pew

I judge that my prayer is more than the devil himself; if it were otherwise, Luther would have fared differently long before this. Yet men will not see and acknowledge the great wonders or miracles God works in my behalf. If I should neglect prayer but a single day, I should lose a great deal of the fire of faith.

—Martin Luther

Before Pentecost, the apostles could only glimpse the great importance of prayer. But the Spirit coming and filling on Pentecost elevated prayer to its vital and all-commanding position in the gospel of Christ. Now the call of prayer to every saint is the Spirit's loudest and most insistent call. Sainthood's piety is made, refined, perfected, by prayer. The gospel moves with slow and timid pace when the saints are not at their prayers early and late and long.

Where are the Christlike leaders who can teach the modern saints how to pray? Where are the apostolic leaders who can set God's people to praying? If they will come to the front and do the work, it will be the greatest work which can be done.

An increase of educational facilities and a great increase of money force will be a curse to religion if not sanctified by more and better praying than we are doing. But more praying will not come as a matter of course. We need a specific effort from praying leadership. The chief ones must lead in the apostolic effort to re-instate the vital importance and practice of prayer in the heart and life of the church.

Only praying leaders will have praying followers. Praying apostles beget praying saints. A praying pulpit will result in praying pews. But we are not a generation of praying saints. Nonpraying Christians are a beggarly gang who have neither the ardor nor the beauty nor the power of saints. The one who can set the church to praying will be the greatest of reformers.

The great need of the church in this and all ages is men and women of commanding faith, of unsullied holiness, of marked spiritual vigor, and consuming zeal. Their prayers, faith, lives, and ministry will be radical and aggressive, working spiritual revolutions in individual lives and in the church.

Such leaders are not those who get up sensational stirs by novel devices, nor those who attract by entertaining. Rather, they stir things up, and work revolutions by the ministry of God's work and the power of the Holy Ghost—revolutions which change the whole current of history.

Natural ability and educational advantage do not figure as factors in this matter. The true spiritual leaders are marked by capacity for faith, the ability to pray, the power of thorough concentration, unselfcenteredness, the loss of self in the glory of God. Such people can set the church ablaze for God, not in a noisy, showy way, but with an intense and quiet heat that melts and moves everything for God.

God can work wonders if he can get a suitable servant. People can work wonders if they can get God to lead them. The full endowment of the Spirit that turned the world upside down at Pentecost would be eminently useful in these days. Men and women who can stir things for God, whose spiritual influences change the whole aspect of life, are the universal need of the church.

The church has never been without these people; they adorn its history. They are the standing miracles attesting to the divinity of their Lord; their example and history are an unfailing inspiration and blessing.

But the church that is dependent upon its past history for its miracles of power and grace is a fallen church. That which has been done in spiritual matters can be done again, and be better done. This was Christ's view. He said, "Verily, verily, I say unto you, He that believeth on me, the works that I do shall he do also; and greater works than these shall he do; because I go unto my Father" (John 14:12). The past has not exhausted the possibilities nor the demands for doing great things in Christ's name.

God wants men and women devoid of self and the world by a severe crucifixion; men and women cleared of self by a bankruptcy which has so totally ruined self and the world that there is neither hope nor desire of recovery. Those who, through prayer, are emptied by such insolvency and crucifixion, turn toward God with perfect hearts.

Questions for Personal Insight and Group Discussion

1.   What hindrances stand in the way of the kind of powerful and effective prayer manifested on the day of Pentecost?

2.   Bounds says, "God can work wonders if he can get a suitable servant." What is a "suitable servant" in God's eyes? How am I included in that roster?

3.   Is the church today "dependent upon its past history for its miracles of power and grace"? How? What can be done to change that tendency?

4.   What does it mean to have a "perfect heart" toward God? How can my prayer life help me toward that goal?